T0153718

COMPUTER AIDED RESEARCH
IN NEAR EASTERN STUDIES:

AN INTRODUCTION

The primary purpose of this new journal is the dissemination of tools for the use of electronic data processing in the various disciplines which deal with the Near East. It is natural, of course, that many of the results obtained in this area would also be of interest for other areas of the humanities and the social sciences.

General and methodological considerations will preferably be accompanied by practical implementations. There are many reasons for this orientation of CARNES. First, our disciplines have a real need for the development of tools that might free the scholar from laborious clerical tasks: these tend sometimes to acquire greater primacy than analysis and to emerge as an end in itself. Second, we wish to serve a paedagogical end, in helping all interested scholars in developing a higher degree of computer literacy. Third - and lest the other two points may seem too modest - we hope that the effect of the quantitative progress more clearly in evidence in computer related work will in the end provoke profound changes in the quality itself of the research, in the sense proposed by J. C. Gardin ("La logique du plausible," Paris 1981).

In this spirit, it is necessary that the scholar be in a position to access the new tools and to adapt them to specific needs without necessarily having to pass through the intermediary of technical personnel or specialized institutions. This is why a good part of the material covered in CARNES will be especially geared to micro-computers, which are more and more within reach of everyone - economically, technically, and ... psychologically.

In the same spirit, the programs which we will publish will be presented in a style which is totally transparent, with commentaries which are conceived for readers whose knowledge of the "exact" sciences may be somewhat tenuous. This approach is an expansion of the concept, traditional in data processing, of program documentation. While such a documentation is often the last step taken (if ever!) by programmers, it will become a first priority in the case of CARNES. Thus any user with a modicum of expertise in programming will be able not only to understand the logic of the programs presented, but also to modify, adapt and hopefully improve them.

For all the emphasis on data processing, there will be an equivalent stress on the nature and quality of the substantive issues addressed. CARNES is not just a data processing journal, it is just as much a journal in the service of the various disciplines dealing with the Near East. Data processing systems and applications must be presented with a view toward this orientation: the pertinent substantive issues must be described, and the relevance of the particular system or application must be shown. This is not only a conceptual presupposition of an editorial nature, it is also a reflection of the paedagogical orientation of CARNES: users are more likely to appreciate a technique and to learn it if the substantive relevance is clearly documented.

In line with our concerns for accessibility of data processing to the field of Near Eastern studies, we plan to start in the near future a special service for a more individualized follow-up of certain topics and areas of interest. This service will deal with both systems and applications and will provide some degree of personal feedback for readers who have implemented on their own equipment the programs published in CARNES.

The hardware utilized in support of any particular software application will always be identified in detail, where necessary even with information on costs, supply sources and support facilities. This is in order to make it as easy as possible for a potential user to adopt some of the systems described. In order to minimize problems of compatibility, we encourage the use of languages easily accessible on standard equipment, especially Pascal and BASIC. Whenever possible, it may prove useful to give alternative instructions for utilization of the same program on different versions of the same languages.

The distribution of pertinent materials in magnetic media is of course acceptable as part of CARNES. Modalities and specifications will be defined in the measure in which the various articles warrant it. We will also give bibliographical information, a bulletin on available hardware, a bulletin on current research, etc. The format of the system of Monographic Journals of the Near East seems especially suited for a flexible style of presentation, a rapid rhythm of publication and a ready adaptation to the diverse needs of the many disciplines dealing with the Near East.

G. B. and O. R.

Monographic Journals of the Near East   CARNES 1/1 (September 1983)

Terqa Preliminary Reports, No. 12:

DIGITAL PLOTTING
OF ARCHAEOLOGICAL FLOOR PLANS

by
Giorgio Buccellati
and
Olivier Rouault

ABSTRACT

A computer program for digital plotting of archaeological
floor plans was implemented during the 8th season of
excavations at Terqa (Spring 1983). This article describes
first the nature of the archaeological questions involved -
precision of the record, ease of access to the data, logistic
efficiency. There is then a listing of the main program
with a detailed commentary and sample outputs; two
special utility programs are also included. The programs
are written in BASIC and are operational on a TRS-80
Model 100 (Portable Computer) with a plotter TRS-80
Model FP215.

TABLE OF CONTENTS

LIST OF FIGURES

1. GENERAL BACKGROUND

For the first time during the 1982 season (TQ7), a microcomputer was introduced in the field at Terqa for the analysis of stratigraphic data.(*) The results of the work done during the 1982 season led to a thorough revision of our encoding system. The new system was implemented experimentally in the following season (TQ8, Spring 1983), and is currently being prepared systematically for publication as a new edition of the IIMAS Field Encoding Manual. The emphasis in our approach has been primarily on stratigraphic, as different from typological, analysis. The data are keyed to quick sorting and retrieval according to categories which are very specifically stratigraphic: in this sense a computer operation in the field is not a luxury, as it might perhaps be considered when it is used only to anticipate typological work. Stratigraphic information has direct and immediate bearing on the research strategy of day to day operations; also, verification of stratigraphic data

---

(*) The Joint Expedition to Terqa is sponsored by the University of California at Los Angeles, the California State University - Los Angeles, IIMAS - The International Institute for Mesopotamian Area Studies, the University of Rome, the Centre National des Recherches Scientifiques - Paris, the University of Arizona, Johns Hopkins University. It is under the direction of Giorgio Buccellati and Marilyn Kelly-Buccellati, with Mario Liverani as Associate Director. Support for the excavations has come through major grants from AICF - the Ambassador International Cultural Foundation, the S. H. Kress Foundation, the Ahmanson Foundation, the American Schools of Oriental Research. A special equipment grant for the research described in this article came from the Neutrogena Corporation.

If the logistic conditions for work in the field were as positive as we report below it is due in large measure to the climate of scholarly cooperation which makes archaeological field work in Syria such an enriching experience. For their unfailing support in this direction we wish to express our gratitude to all our colleagues of the Directorate General of Antiquities and Museums who, under the leadership of Dr. A. Behnassi, are to be credited for the current flourishing of archaeology in Syria.

input is often possible only if the work is still in progress and the pertinent evidence has not been removed. Typological information, on the other hand, is more independent of the excavation moment as such, especially for movable artifacts, hence its utilization in computerized format is less urgent for field utilization. Not that typological computerization is unimportant - quite the contrary. There are certainly incalculable benefits to be reaped from a typological data base which can be utilized in the field: the identification of typological traits, for instance, may help in providing chronological points of reference for an assemblage and therefore a stratum; it may also shed light on the functional value of an artifact and thereby explain certain emplacement characteristics of the general stratigraphic setting. The emphasis on stratigraphy, therefore, is not meant to belittle the importance of typology for field work. It rather aims at stressing the fact that proper stratigraphic data entry can only be done in the field, and that in turn the gratest utilization of a stratigraphic data base comes during the moment of excavation itself. Hence the qualitative difference that computer aided stratigraphic analysis can make for field work itself.

Along these lines of reasoning, a new dimension of field oriented computer work was introduced at Terqa in the 1983 season (TQ8) - graphic plotting. The general presupposition was that digital plotting should improve statigraphic recording in the field, from the moments of observation and verification to the moments of recording and evaluation. In other words, the test for the validity of a field plotting system should be that (1) the attention is in fact channeled more directly toward the data; (2) verification and eventual corrections can be introduced rapidly; (3) the consequent recording is more accurate and more highly differentiated; (4) the data can be easily accessed in their differentiated state. To put it yet more concretely: (1) can we observe initially more data if we have the support of a digital plotting system? (2) can we maintain a clean set of data, or are we going to drown in a mass of unverified figures? (3) can we control the more minute aspects of the recording, or are we going to lose sight of the essential? and (4) can we make enough use of retrieval possibilities to yield adequate returns on the initial investment of resources?

Borne out of direct field experience, our answer to these questions is positive, and this article is our attempt at documenting it. The experiment in the field, which was concluded only two months prior to the writing of this article, served to prove the following: the hardware is sufficiently reliable even under relatively difficult conditions; the logistics of data input and retrieval is within reach of the general staff at the site; and the whole application of digital plotting represents a major qualitative improvement in the nature of the recording. The software implementation available in the field in TQ8 was still not adequate for a full operationalization of the system, but it was enough to allow us to develop the software package presented here in the short period following the field season.

Of the two authors of this paper, G. Buccellati has contributed the general research design, the definition of the field goals and the preliminary programming which was used in the field, while O. Rouault, in collaboration with G. Buccellati, has contributed the program design and the operational programming. Previous to the excavation season of TQ8, Darryl Rothering had developed an alternative program for use with the TRS Color Computer. This program is highly interactive and contains features not included in our present programs: it was however temporarily set aside because the amount of memory it required for proper functioning made it more difficult to use for field implementation. The aspects of field surveying and the special system for the computation of coordinates (see below, Sections 2 and 3) were developed under the supervision of Stephen M. Hughey; a separate fascicle of the Terqa Preliminary Reports is currently in preparation detailing these aspects of the project.

The scope of this article is primarily practical. We wish to make available the methods and techniques which would enable field archaeologists working in similar conditions to utilize the same system. We will address questions of an archaeological nature to the extent that they will help to understand the functioning of the system and its goals. It must be noted that the system is still preliminary and that several refinements are possible and, in fact, intended. It must also be noted that we expect a minimum of acquaintance with programming in BASIC; however, rather detailed explanations of the program are included, so that users with even a small amount of programming experience may be able on the one hand to use the program as a self-teaching device, and on the other to easily enter general improvements or specific modifications to suit their own particular needs.

2. ARCHAEOLOGICAL BACKGROUND

While every metric grid utilized on an excavation is potentially a centimetric grid, the actual degree of accuracy which can be obtained varies considerably depending on circumstantial factors. Some of the limitations are as follows. (1) The actual measurements taken initially in the field may fall short of centimetric precision. Leaving aside accidental factors, there are built-in, systemic hitches which may be a cause. Line levels, for instance have a high incidence of error in measuring elevations for distances greater than one or two meters. (2) The measurements taken are recorded not in digital, but rather in analogical form. This happens typically when a distance measured from a control point is transferred on graph paper by means of a compass or other similar device, without being recorded on a numeric log. (3) The initial measurement and the attendant recording may in fact be accurate, but retrieving the information is so difficult that the initial accuracy is practically lost, because it cannot be correlated to all other pertinent data.

To obtain an effective centimetric grid one has to overcome these problems. The first problem is partly to be resolved through better recording equipment, and partly through a more rigorous application of systemic controls. At Terqa, much attention has been devoted to both aspects of the problem, especially with the collaboration of S. Hughey, and a full report is in preparation on the subject (Stratigraphic surveying, forthcoming in TPR).

The second and third problem can best be obviated by the utilization of digital plotting. Digital plotting is built in the first place on digital information, which it retains in a very precise and rigorous format; the analogical or graphic translation of the digital information is produced through a transposition of digital information which is not only much more accurate than any manual rendering, but is also newly generated each time from identical digital information: any new copy or generation has exactly the same degree of accuracy as the earlier ones, without the danger of attrition through manual graphic transposition. Digital plotting is thus both digital and analogical in a way that cannot be claimed by any other plotting.

This virtual identity of digital and analogical representation of the data is at the same time the key for the solution to the third problem - ease of access to even the most minute of information. Graphic representation is in this sense nothing more than an index to numerical values, an index which allows quick access to those values. Graphic renderings of the data can be produced at any scale starting from the same digital information. A multi-scale representation is like a multi-tiered system, which allows for diversified retrieval without any compromise with the initial amount of data collected. The digital information is always available in its entirety, and the graphic rendering provides the interpolations which are useful for a proper understanding of relations. In other words, graphic or analogical renderings highlight the relationships among terminal points (the digital bits of information), but these same bits are retained in their original integrity so that the relation can be questioned and evaluated afresh at any time.

If the record of absolute space distribution is the main goal of stratigraphic recording, digital plotting provides the best approach to its implementation. The absolute numerical values are retained forever as an integral part of the system, but their relationship to any other numerical value is always immediately accessible in a true volumetric perspective, i.e. in a three-dimensional sense.

Digital plotting is then much more than just an easier way to produce results which could be produced just as well, if less easily, manually. It is not just a technological luxury. The ease of formatting the information makes for a much greater ease of retrieval; as a result, comparisons at different levels of analysis are more easily done, and the consequent analysis is correspondingly improved. Ultimately, more information will in fact be gathered and recorded in the first place if there is a more direct and capillary feedback as soon as the new information is added to the old one. Verification of the data becomes a part of the process of analysis itself, rather than just a clerical proofreading of disconnected bits of information.

The emphasis on proper stratigraphic controls is in line with a general understanding, characteristic of the Terqa project, of "archaeology as archaeology," i. e. as a discipline with a set of normative procedures and methodologies all its own. Stratigraphic analysis is the hallmark of this intellectual autonomy of archaeology: it is the only task for which the archaeologist borrows from no other disciplines, at least not in a direct way. There seems to be a general consensus that stratigraphic methods and techniques currently in use are adequate: this is reflected in the almost total lack of current literature on the subject, from either a theoretical or a practical perspective. In point of fact, however, the degree of objectivity in stratigraphic analysis is very limited: ironically, the vast intellectual structures which are being built along interpretive lines take for granted a set of data which is itself much less tested and "scientific" than the interpretations it gives rise to. The standard for acceptable stratigraphic material is derived ultimately from the logic of the argument presented and from the reputation of the excavators rather than from independently testable and well documented classes of evidence. The effort of the Terqa project in this direction is intended to serve the needs of an improved approach to stratigraphic analysis, and the elements of digital plotting presented in this article are an important contribution in this direction.

The results presented here are useful within the context of a concrete and immediate field implementation. They are however preliminary in two respects. On

CARNES 1,7

the one hand, various refinements are possible and intended from the point of view of data processing techniques: these will be described below. On the other hand, there are also several projections in terms of archaeological analysis. In particular, we plan to work in the future on the implementation of (1) automatic sections cut at will through any plane of the deposition; (2) three-dimensional sections which may be related to the data-base information and provide a graphic flowchart of the depositional process (an equivalent of the Harris matrix, but with a much higher degree of resolution); (3) elevations and reconstructions for architectural components; (4) interface with a disk and data base system for faster retrieval of files. We hope to develop these plans in close conjunction with research being done within the framework of architectural studies: archaeology has not made sufficient use of this discipline except in a very practical sense (many of the leading Near Eastern archaeologists were in fact trained as architects). And yet there is one fundamental similarity which touches at the core of the intellectual effort in both disciplines: while archaeology aims at reconstructing function from the observation of spacial relationships, so architecture aims, conversely, at arranging spacial relationship on the basis of known functional needs. Both deal with the organization of space and its relationship to individual and social needs. Both deal, as it has been eloquently pointed out by D. Preziosi, with the "semiotics of the built environment" ("The Semiotics of the Built Environment: An Introduction to Architectonic Analysis," Bloomington 1979). The technical support and the expertise already available within the framework of architecture as a discipline and a profession is much more developed than for archaeology, and it is to be hoped that a collaboration in that direction may be of direct benefit to the type of archaeological concerns expressed in this article.

3. DATA PROCESSING BACKGROUND

Hardware

The main components of the graphic system in use at Terqa are a TRS-80 Model 100 Portable Computer with 31 K of memory and a TRS-80 Model FP215 Flatbed Plotter; for data storage, a standard cassette recorder was used. (A second computer, which has been in use since 1982, is a larger disk system; this, however, has not been used for graphic work, but only for data processing. Interface between the two is a task for the future.) This configuration of the system costs around $2000. In terms of both quality and costs, this is a middle of the line configuration, although less expensive systems would probably be much less effective.

A matrix printer was used for program listings (matrix printers are available in a wide range of prices). The matrix printer is however not indispensable, because the plotter does reproduce program listings even if very slowly, and it also prints normal text files (with the help of a utility program, see below, Section 8); the program listings given below in Section 8 were printed on the plotter.

The Portable Computer Model 100 came on the market only a couple of weeks before we left for the field, and for this reason it could be used initially merely as a back-up system. (The main system in the beginning was a TRS-80 Color Computer. This had been used in Los Angeles previous to the 1983 season in preparing for the field work, and for this reason it was taken to the field. Once the software adaptations were made, there was no question as to the excellent suitability of the Portable Computer Model 100 for our purposes, and it is the one now in normal use.) The Model 100 is a very small unit, about the size of a large book, with a good version of BASIC and a modest but effective word processor built in (accessible through ROM beyond the 31K of available RAM memory). It runs on 4 AA batteries (as well as on AC), which makes it extremely convenient for a field situation where the power supply is not fully dependable. Typically, the data would be entered on the portable unit and then stored on cassettes, using a tape recorder which also runs on batteries. (The Portable Computer came to be used regularly by all staff members also for the prose version of the daily journal. It is our intention in the future to have two or more Portable Computers in the field to use as regular data entry stations for all our data, graphic and otherwise; data base entries will then be converted to the larger disk system, also available at Terqa, for computational procedures.)

One advantage of a plotting system is that it can be treated as a system of text files, so that a disk system is not necessary. While a disk is indispensable, for instance, for large sorts, in the case of plotted information sorts can easily be done in a sequential fashion, much like chapters in a text file. Hence storage of the large files on tape is adequate, and an internal memory of 31K, or even 24 K, is also adequate for intermediate operations. The limited loss of speed and file size is an acceptable trade-off vis-a-vis the advantages of price, reliability (the unit is more compact than any disc system), availability of supplies (batteries, tape-recorders, cassette tapes are available even in Bedouin tents) and logistics (power supply, portability).

For the computation of coordinate values from ties (see below, Section 4) a program was developed as part of the Color Computer software package designed by Darryl Rothering. During the 1983 season we have however relied on two Texas Instruments TI58C with commercially available surveying software. This approach may in fact be continued because it provides for a better utilization of the available resources: the less expensive TI unit is used to compute coordinates while the Portable Computer is used to enter other data. In view of the need to use the equipment every day for a number of different operations by different staff members and only during a limited amount of time after the excavations, such practical considerations are important. More significantly, the TI model is used regularly on the excavation itself and thus allows immediate and direct verification of the derived measurements.

The choice of the TRS-80 hardware was initially conditioned by the price range, which was a considerable factor for an experimental investment. It turned out to be quite satisfactory in terms of reliability under field conditions, and the introduction of the Portable Computer added a major quality consideraton. For the purposes of this article, this will be the only hardware considered. We expect, however, to develop further our research in the near future, and to introduce at that point variations which will make the system compatible with various other types of hardware, and especially with a disk system.

CARNES 1,9

Plotter vs. Matrix Printer

The obvious main advantage of a matrix printer is the speed of operation, and the obvious advantage of a plotter is the quality of the graphic rendering. There are however other considerations which affect the needs of a field operation like the one envisaged here.

(1) Small, calculator size matrix printers are available which can provide a graphic rendering of coordinates at the excavation itself (this is hardly possible with a plotter); the advantage in this case is the possibility of obtaining a quick readout for visual control, to check for obvious mistakes of measurement. Both the hardware alternatives and the software applications which are pertinent to this utilization will be described in a forthcoming TPR fascicle ("Stratigraphic surveying").

(2) All lines on a plotted plan, whether drawn by an architect or by a mechanical plotter, are in fact extrapolations from points which have been measured in the ground. By definition, the precision of digital measurements extends only to the points themselves: the connecting lines are the result of standardization and extrapolation, which are introduced analogically from visual inspection. A plotted plan produced by a mechanical plotter may be deceptive in this respect, if it suggests a rigidity in the resulting configuration which is not actually in the data themselves. The advantage of a dot rather than a line configuration is that it requires manual extrapolation. This requirement can easily be met by producing with the graphic plotter an alternate version with dots instead of full lines. On the other hand, the time taken by hand drawing may be avoided in intermediate generations of the plotted plan by having a segmented line which indicates a degree of approximation.

There are many advantages to a mechanical plotter which cannot be underestimated. For one, a regularized line is in fact acceptable in most instances, especially if there are sufficient points measured. Second, color lines can be used very effectively to indicate differences in the data. Third, and most importantly, the possibility of selection from a number of categories makes it possible to sort data in a number of different ways and in a representation style which is truly analogical and therefore immediately accessible: for instance, a rendering of only the structural elements from a certain stratum may be reproduced rapidly and verified easily against the data; automatic reduction to different scales may allow the comparisons of different excavation units placed side by side; etc.

Software

The choice of BASIC as a language, while not the best in terms of ultimate graphic potentials, seems well justified in terms of its ease of utilization. It is the language with which all beginners are familiar, and it is well supported by all microcomputer systems: adaptation to such systems is therefore quite easy. Some of the akward aspects of our software depend from the nature of the language, and must thus be viewed and hopefully accepted in the light of the above considerations.

The format of the program presented below (AFP1) is rather diffused in order to make it more easily understandable to users. A more compact format may be desirable in other respects (from memory space to elegance of the logical system) but would make the program itself less transparent, especially for users who are not experienced programmers. Now one of the purposes of this article (and in fact of the journal it inaugurates) is precisely to make programs as widely accessible as possible, so that they may serve the double purpose of providing a realistic outlet for substantive research while at the same time helping in the process of program training, which is in fact largely self-training.

There still remains of course much that can be improved even within the disclaimers given above. We do expect to present later versions of the program which may upgrade the system and provide alternatives. The current value, however, is primarily in the fact that, whatever its shortcoming, this is a functioning system which has been tested in the field and is currently operational.

4. THE DATA

The basic data consist of volumetric "Relays" (R). These are points which are triangulated in function of a system of preset horizontal and vertical points. In other words, they are measured according to a three-dimensional array so that each point is defined by three measurements. Each measurement is a "tie" (i. e. distance) from one of many established and fixed "Control Points."

Control points are of two types: the horizontal control points (HP or H) are tied to an horizontal grid (i. e. a two-dimensional array), the vertical control points (VP or V) are tied to a single vertical axis. Horizontal control points are defined by two figures which correspond to points on the N and the E coordinates; vertical control points are listed sequentially on a bar which is set perpendicular to the plane of the horizontal grid. These points are part of a network of volumetric controls which are regularly found on all excavations, and which have to be set and maintained by a trained surveyor; for the purposes of this article, the general procedure involving these types of volumetric controls is assumed as a known fact; more information about specific aspects of the Terqa system of volumetric controls will be found in a forthcoming TPR fascicle on "Stratigraphic Surveying."

The ties are entered on a log sheet (see Fig. 3a). Each relay point is defined by two required ties (to two different fixed horizontal control points) and by one optional tie (to one vertical control point). Relay points are numbered sequentially within a "Volumetric Reference Log," and can be referred to by such numbers. (Some measurements are derived not from control points, but from other known points. The second entry line in the log sheet for each relay is used to enter these measurements when applicable. For the purposes of the present argumentation this aspect of the recording system may be disregarded. It will be discussed in detail in the forthcoming article on stratigraphic surveying.)

From such ties, coordinates are derived through preset programs (either with the TI Model 58C or with a program on the main computing package); also, elevations are derived through simple arithmetics. Coordinates and elevations are entered on the log sheet (see Fig. 3a).

The relay points, defined by means of coordinates and elevations, are clustered in sequences which correspond to individual features found in the excavations (e. g. a

CARNES 1,11

wall or an object). This sequence is important in that it defines the configuration which emerges from the appropriate correlation of the points.

It is then these points and their internal sequence which constitute the input data for the plotting programs. The following diagram summarizes the main components of our data in terms of the horizontal system of measurements:

RELAY POINT

tie - HP (horiz. control point)
tie - HP (horiz. control point)
} — North and East coordinates

tie - VP (vert. control point) —— elevation

5. INPUT: DATA FILES

Archaeological aspects of format

The data are included in text files that have an identical format in terms of data processing but may differ at will in terms of archaeological content.

Archaeologically, there are primarily two types of files. In one type, called Graphic Archive, data are categorized according to their stratigraphic and typological definition - e.g. a wall of a given stratum, a tablet of given content. In the Terqa encoding system, there are two major categories of stratigraphic elements, "Stationary Units" or "Features" (F) and "Movable Items" (M). One of these two letters, followed by a number identifies uniquely any unit from area to area and from season to season. 8F1103, for instance, may identify such a feature as a wall, and the label is resolved as follows:

    8 : 8th season (Terqa is not included in the label)
    F : feature
    1 : volume 1 of the recording system
    103 : sequential number of features within volume 1.

For the purpose of a file name, only the label F103 is used: both the season and the volume are presumed in the cassette on which the data are stored. (The full label may however be entered, if desired, in the data file itself.) Files, then, might be of the type **Fnnn** or **Mnnn** (F for Feature or M for Movable Item followed by a number up to three digit long). See Figs. 5-6 for sample entries from the Graphic Archive.

The other type of file is the Graphic Journal. Here the area excavated on a given day is plotted, with the inclusion of all the relay points measured on that day. The area excavated on the previous day(s) is normally also included, but selectively; color codes indicate the different days. See Fig. 3b for a sample entry.

These files are for all practical purposes to .be considered as text files. So for instance, they can be merged, copied, subdivided at will, depending on the particular purpose of the archaeologist, and they can be stored in any of these configurations.

Computer aspects of format

In the Model 100, data files are opened as regular text files (with a suffix .DO). They consist of a sequence of lines, such as the one shown in Fig. 4. Each line contains an instruction or command for the graphic plotter. The commands may be divided into three groups depending on whether they have a letter followed by one, or two, or several figures. A summary of the codes used is found in Fig. 1.

Only one command requires no additional figures, the command **H**, which sends the pen to the "home" position, i.e. the lower left corner of the plotter.

Single Figure Command

These are commands which control variable graphic parameters in the plotter. A summary with graphic rendering for each code is found in Fig. 2. The ones which are in common use are as follows (note that all commands must be in upper case letters; the lower case letters used in the formulas below refer to digits):

L0 for solid line: this is used for an observed line
L1 for dotted line; the length of each segment in the dotted line is controlled by a command which follows L1, in the form **Bnnn**; the formats which are in common use for dotted lines are
      B7 = small dots : segmented curve or wavy line
      B10 = small dashes : reconstructed line
      B20 = dashes : excavation line
      B200 = long segments : volumetric line

Snnn for size of printed numbers and letters; the sizes in common use are:
      S2 for log number of Volumetric Relays
      S4 for label of stratigraphic units
      S6 for title of page.

      Note that if the values of L and S are not specified, the last value entered will function by default as the current value.

N0 for small x mark : to indicate elevation
N3 for small triangle : to indicate findspot of small movable item

Double Figure Commands

These commands move the pen on the page to points defined by specific coordinates: in each case, the two figures correspond to the two coordinates. Note that from a surveying point of view, the first coordinate is always the North coordinate (vertical), and the second the East coordinate (horizontal). From a mathematical point of views, on the other hand, the first coordinate is always the X axis (horizontal), and the second the Y axis (horizontal). The Texas Instruments Model 58C calculates the coordinates from a surveying point of view, while the plotter defines them mathematically: this simply means that of a pair of numbers entered in the plotter, the first one must always be the East coordinate, and the second the North coordinate.

There are only two double figure commands used in our program:

Mxxxx,yyyy moves the pen to the point defined by the two coordinates (x and y respectively, or East and North), without drawing a line;

Dxxxx,yyyy draws a straight line from the point where the pen is currently located to the point defined by the two coordinates written after the command D.

For the purposes of the present plotting system, coordinates are defined in terms of a frame which corresponds to an excavation unit 10 meters on the side. Each excavation unit is defined by a set of four digits which correspond to the first two digits of the North and the East axis respectively. Thus Excavation Unit 3554 is framed by a square whose Southwestern corner corresponds to a point defined by the coordinates 350 meters North and 540 meters East. (Note that the 0,0 point for the site is located at some distance to the southwest of the site.) Every set of coordinates plotted will assume as 0,0 the lower left corner of the frame, and all coordinates are in centimeters. This procedure allows shorter numbers to be entered in the data file: while the full coordinates might be 35603 cms. North and 55450 cms. East, we need only enter 450 for the X axis and 603 for the Y axis: this will locate the point precisely within the frame, which is in turn located on the overall site grid by the label 3554.

Multi-Figure Command

Circles and arcs are defined by a special command which has the following configuration:

Cxxxx,yyyy,rrr,bbb,eee

x and y are digits which refer to the appropriate coordinates of the center of the circle;

r is the length of the radius in centimeters;

b is the beginning of the arc, and e is the end of the arc in angles. A full circle is defined by a beginning angle 0 and an end angle 360. Any intermediate angle will define a section of a circle, i.e. an arc: examples are shown in Fig. 2b.

The definition of the two extremities of the arc is not obtained mathematically, but rather manually according to the following procedure. The full circle is drawn of which the arc is a part: the circle will intersect pre-existing lines, which will mark the extremities of the arc -- such as with a pit cutting into a wall. At this point a transparent template with the appropriate grid marked on it, or some similar tool for itdentifying coordinates, is placed on the plotted drawing, and the coordinate values of the intersections are noted; these are then entered at the appropriate place in the arc formula. While far from sophisticated, this procedure has the advantage of providing a relatively easy type of input sufficient for a field situation.

6. OUTPUT: PLOTTING OPERATIONS

Once the data files are created, they are accessed by the program called AFP1 (Archaeological Floor Plans, N. 1). The flow chart of the program, together with a summary of the most important commands, is given in Fig. 1.

Definitions of graphic parameters.

As the program begins, it prompts for the following information:

```
Enter orientation code (v or h)
?
```

The code "v" will orient all plotting in a vertical direction: this is the normal orientation for pages which include a normal excavation unit and are then entered in the field books. The horizontal orientation ("h") is useful for special formats, such as larger areas of excavation shown on a smaller scale. There is no default value for this entry: a wrong key, including a capital V or H, will bring back the prompt on the screen.
The next choice affects the point of origin for the coordinates which will be entered, i. e. the point which will serve as 0,0 for all subsequent coordinates. This is in practice the lower left corner of the frame, hence the prompt reads:

```
Enter coordinates for lower left corner
   - X coordinate: ?
   - Y coordinate: ?
```

The digits entered are the last three digits (i.e. the meters and centimeters) of the East coordinate for the X axis, and the last three digits of the North coordinate for

the Y axis. As noted earlier, there is an inversion in standard sequence between surveying and mathematical practices. The point of origin thus established will serve as 0,0 for all subsequent coordinates, as follows:
every positive X value will be to the right of the point of origin;
every negative X value will be to the left of the point of origin;
every positive Y value will be above the point of origin;
every negative Y value will be below the pint of origin.
The next choice pertains to the scale at which the plotting is to be done. Data are normally entered at a 1:100 scale, which corresponds to about one fourth of a normal page. To fill the page with one excavation unit one will choose a scale of 1:50, while higher scales will be for special conditions. The prompt reads:

```
Enter scale factor:
   - Operator (/ or *)        ?
   - Any number 0.1 to 20     ?
```

The term "operator" refers to the type of computation one wishes to perform: / stands for division, and * stands for multiplication. The number which follows is the factor to be used in the computation. By default, the values will be /1, which yields a scale of 1:100. The limits of 0.1 to 20 have been chosen arbitrarily, as defining a normal range for the type of operations performed in the field. The common factors are as follows:
/4 : scale 1:400
/2 : scale 1:200
/1 : scale 1:100
*2 : scale 1:50
*4 : scale 1:25
*10: scale 1:10

The next prompt asks for a definition of the quality or density of the curved lines:

```
Enter step factor for curve:
   - Any number 0.1 to 5       ?
```

There is a correlation between quality and speed which accounts for the presence of this special parameter. With a low value, the line is in fact segmented rather than curve (this is especially noticeable in cases where the radius is small); the speed of execution is however greater. The inverse is true with higher values: at the maximum of the range allowed (a maximum which has been chosen arbitrarily) the line is defined by dots which are so close together as to produce a really curved line, but it takes proportionately longer to execute. Typically, then, lower values will be used for interim runs, and higher values for final copy. By default, the value is set at 0.5.

The final prompt of this series defines the size of the print characters:

```
Enter print size
   - Any number 1 to 25        ?
```

This command is identical to that already described under the formula **Snnn** above in the preceding section. Print size parameters included in the data files overrule those defined interactively. The interactive definition available at this point is thus to be used for data files which include alphanumeric characters without a definition of size; such a procedure is generally preferable, partly because one can thus reduce the amount of data entry in the files, and partly to have greater formatting freedom at the moment of plotting. The range 1-25 is arbitrarily set in function of normal plotting operations in the field. By default, the value is set at 3.

Handling of data files.

At this point, the execution of the program branches out in three parallel directions. The prompt reads:

```
Full files or single entries?
   - f (full files)
   - s (single entries)
   - k (from keyboard)
     ?
```

The first and second options call up the same prompt:

```
List files to plot, as follows:
      filename          - for central memory
      CAS:filename      - for files on cassette
      end               - to exit current pass
If from cassette, check recorder!
?
```

At this point, the names of the files desired are entered sequentially, up to a maximum of 20. Files in central memory need not be entered in any sequence; files on tape instead must be entered in the same sequence in which they are stored. Files in central memory need no prefix; files on tape need a prefix CAS:. If from cassette, the tape recorder must be properly connected and in the Play mode. A wrong filename will be discovered when the machine attempts to load it: at that point, a message will flash on the screen, and the program will bring you back to the beginning the file handling process. A mistake in the file input will be discovered when the machine reads through the file during the plotting process: at that point, a message will flash on the screen, and the program will go back to the last prompt.

After the file names have been entered, one must conclude with the word "end"; this will start the plotter in the execution of the commands. The same is obtained by default: pressing carriage return without a file name causes the program to exit the current pass.

The total of 20 files allowed in the first pass was chosen as an average of files to be processed during any one pass. It is preferable not to enter too many in a single pass, in case mistakes are discovered during the execution of the plotting. The end of the first pass provides also an opportunity to change some of the parameters (through the keyboard option, see presently) or to change colors (color change is done manually on the FP215). After the last plotting command is executed, the last prompt appears on the screen:

```
Any additional files? ('y' or 'n')
?
```

A positive answer restarts the file handling process. A negative answer terminates the program.

Direct access.

The option "k" in the first prompt of the data handling process switches operation from a file mode to a direct mode. The prompts, which appear sequentially on the screen as each one is answered, are as follows:

```
Parameters for entry from keyboard:
     - command              ?
     - value or X           ?
     - Y                    ?
     - radius               ?
     - arc,start            ?
     - arc,end              ?
```

These are the same codes explained above in section 5. Impossible values will be rejected. If a mistake is made after the return carriage has been pressed, the code "9999" will cause the prompt to start from the beginning.

The direct access mode is very useful as a means to override certain aspects of the current program without restarting from the beginning. This applies especially to a new definition of the origin or of print size. One can also add information which is missing from the files, for example titles or notes. An important side benefit of the direct access mode is the ability to produce graphics by trial and error, for instance in producing charts. Fig. 1 in this article was produced in this way.

One command may be accessed from the keyboard which is not allowed in the data files, namely **Q**, which controls the rotation of a printed line of characters:

Q0 (which is the normal default value) prints horizontally
Q1 prints vertically from top to bottom
Q2 prints horizontally upside down (from right to left)
Q3 prints vertically from bottom to top.

7. COMMENTARY ON MAIN PROGRAM

What follows is an unusually detailed documentation of the structure and functioning of the program. Such degree of detail constitutes a departure from the norm. What we aim for is an explanation of the program in terms of the substantive data it affects. We hope that this will provide an in depth insight into the program for individuals who have a general knowledge of BASIC: this should explain why certain choices were made, shed light on some of the more complex functions of the language, and enable the user to more easily make adaptations to specific requirements. We hope that this type of program documentation may serve effectively the purposes of a journal like CARNES, and that it may become a regular feature of future articles.

Fixed Definitions

30   establishes an array for file names, limited to 20 positions

40   J = index or counter of current file names

50   I = total number of files

60   speed control for plotter TRS-80 FP215

70   format control for plotter TRS-80 FP215. Note: all commands to plotter are introduced by the word LPRINT.

80   alerts program to existence of a special subroutine which is invoked any time

a general system error is detected by the program

Interactive definitions

110   clears the screen and displays prompt. Note: all prompts are designed for a 40 column, 8 row screen (the size of the TRS-80 Model 100). Spaces as given in the program are important for a proper display effect.

120   defines answer to prompt (through input from keyboard) as a variable OC$ (Orientation Code)

130   rejects answer if it is different from either "v" or "h" and redisplays prompt

140   the plotter TRS-80 FP215 assumes by default an horizontal orientation; thus if the answer is "h," no further command is needed to obtain horizontal plotting; the command Q0 establishes the direction of the alphanumeric writing as horizontal, the command Q3 as vertical. Note: the vertical orientation will be invoked at various points in the program by referring to the value "v" of the variable OC$

200   displays first line of prompt

210   displays second line of prompt and defines answer to prompt as a variable X (X axis)

220   same as 210 for Y axis

230   invokes orientation subroutine if the current orientation is vertical

240   sends command to plotter: if properly connected, and if the pen is not already at the desired point, then the pen will move to the point currently defined on the screen. This point will be the point of origin for all subsequent coordinates

310   displays prompt and expects input from keyboard for variable OP$ (OPerator for scale computation)

320   defines default value of OP$ as "/"; the default value is obtained by pressing any key other than an allowed number, or by pressing carriage return; the default value is displayed at position 70 on the Model 100 screen, i.e. at the place where the normal answer to the prompt would appear

330   displays prompt and expects input from keyboard for variable S (Scale)

340   defines default value of S as "1"; the value established at this point will be invoked later in the program

350-380   analogous to 300-340 **for ST** (curve STep, i.e. line **density**)

390-420   analogous to 300-340 for CS (Character or print Size)

430   the value of CS just established is sent to the plotter, and all subsequent characters will be printed at this size, until a new print size command is entered, either from a file or from the keyboard

Main file pass

450-490   displays prompt and expects input from keyboard for variable SE$ (Single Entry option)

500   invokes subroutine for entry from keyboard

505   ends program upon request

510   defines default value of SE$ as "f" and displays it at the appropriate place on the screen

520-560   displays prompt

570   increments by 1 the index of file sequence (variable I defined in 50), and prevents total from reaching a value higher than 20 (defined in 30 as the maximum for the array)

580   answers to prompt through input from keyboard; the string entered (e.g. F105) is stored in a line of the array N$ (defined in 30); this line receives the current numeric value of I as incremented according to 570 (i.e. each new answer will have an index value higher by 1 vis-a-vis the preceding answer) thereby preventing more than 20 positions to be filled in array N$: if a 21st file name is entered, it is ignored and program exits loop; finally, it allows any new file name to be entered except "end": if "end" is entered, it is not considered as file name, and program exits loop

590   if "end" has been entered in 120, then its sequential value as 1 has also been entered at the same time in the variable I; since "end" is not a file name, its incremental value as 1 is deleted

Data file access

600-840   this loop accesses one file at the time

610   when total number of files has been treated, file counter is reset to 1, value of I is reset to 0 and program exits loop

620   defines data file being treated currently (i.e. the J row of the N$ array)

630   opens current file (i.e. accesses data from data file (e.g. F103)) and defines it as #1 in central memory

Data file handling

700-800   this loop, nested within the preceding loop, handles contents of data file

710   takes current line of current file and defines it as variable XY$; defines a variable PR$ (PRefix) for the first character in XY$ (e.g. M in M200,400))

720-730   if input line contains a character which is not allowed, then the index of files (J) is updated, the file is closed, and program goes back to the file handling prompt

740-760   activates the single entry option: a negative answer, i.e. a value "n" for the variable PO$ (Print Option), bypasses the plotting operation of this particular command, and procedes to the next file entry

770   bypasses the plotting operation if the file entry begins with "*"

780   invokes the subroutine which handles the data from the data file and transforms them into commands for the plotting operation

790   error trap: if the data returned from the subroutine include a "C" then file is closed (this anticipates the eventuality of a defective handling of the entries)

800   sends content of variable XY$ to the plotter

810   if data file is finished, then program exits loop

820   regular end of nested loop

830   regular end of main loop; file counter is incremented by 1, and current file is closed

990   regular end of program

Subroutine: Handling of plotter commands from data file

1010-1180   this subroutine is invoked by 780

1010   clears content of V (Variable), if any

1020-1030   defines V as position of comma in string

1040   if there is no comma in current line of current file, then program exits subroutine; current line is sent without modification to plotter. This takes care of all single figure commands (see above, section 5), which do not involve coordinates

1050   defines variable C1$ (Character 1, i.e. first element in coordinate string) as first character of current line of current file if such line contains a comma (e.g. it isolates M from M400,800)

1060-70   if character isolated is either M or D, the subroutine continues

1080   if character isolated is I, and the orientation is horizontal, the contents are sent back to 780 without further manipulation

1085   if character isolated is I, and the orientation is vertical, the orientation subroutine is invoked, then program returns to data handling bypassing scale reduction or magnification

1090   if character isolated is C, then program goes to circle subroutine and exits current subroutine (first RETURN); if character isolated is any other character, then program exits subroutine and returns to 780 (second RETURN)

1100   defines variable C2$ (i.e. second element in coordinate string) as character to the left of the comma (e.g. M400 in M400,800)

1110   redefines variable C2$ by eliminating first character (400)

1120   defines variable C3$ (i.e. third element in coordinate string) as characters to the right of comma (800)

1130   redefines alphanumeric content of variable C2$ and C3$ as numeric variables labeled X and Y. This procedure is necessary in order to be able to multiply and divide the values of the coordinates by the desired scale factor

1140   invokes orientation subroutine if current orientation is vertical

1150   divides coordinates by scale factor

1160   multiplies coordinates by scale factor

1170 reconstitutes plotter commands in the form of a character string, which is the format required by plotter

1180   regular end of subroutine

Circle/Arc subroutine

2010-2590   this subroutine is invoked by 1090

2010   isolates first part of string to the left of first comma (e.g. C400 in

CARNES 1,23

C400,800,200,90,360)

2020   isolates first letter of string (C)

2030   defines as C3$ the second part of the string to the right of the first comma
        (800,200,90,360)

2040   computes position of first comma in C3$

2050   redefines as C4$ the right portion of C3$ starting from first comma
        (200,90,360)

2060   redefines C3$ as the left portion of the previous C3$ beginning from the first
        comma (800)

2070   computes position of first comma in C4$

2080   defines as C5$ the right portion of C4$ starting from the first comma (90,360)

2090   redefines C4$ as the left portion of the previous C4$ (200)

2100   computes position of comma in C5$

2110   defines C6$ as the right portion of C5$ starting from the comma (360)

2120   redefines C5$ as the left portion of the previous C5$ (90)

2130   transforms the alphanumeric content of C2$, C3$, C4$, C5$ and C6$ in
        numeric values as follows:
        C2$ = X (horizontal or X axis)
        C3$ = V (vertical or Y axis)
        C4$ = R (Radius)
        C5$ = S1 (beginning angle of arc)
        C6$ = S2 (ending angle of arc)

2140   invokes orientation subroutine for coordinates of center of circle if current
        orientation is vertical

2150   bypasses reorientation of angles if arc is a full circle

2160   invokes orientation subroutine for angles if current orientation is vertical; this
        is also the beginning of a subroutine invoked in 5390

2170   divides coordinates and radius by scale factor

2180   multiplies coordinates and radius by scale factor

2190   sets line parameter for circle line to solid line

2500-2580   circle algorithm

2590   regular end of circle/arc subroutine: program returns to 1090 (first RETURN) and to 780 (second RETURN)

Orientation subroutines

3010-20 this subroutine for origin is invoked by 230, 1145 and 5230

3020   sets variable XX to value 2700 (this is the numeric value which on the TRS-80 FP215 plotter corresponds to the lower left corner of an 8 1/2 x 11 page held vertically); sets variable IV (Independent Variable) to current value of X variable; redefines X variable as being equal to 2700 minus the current value of X; redefines Y variable as being equal to IV (i.e. previous value of X); exits subroutine

3100-10 this subroutine for coordinates is invoked by 1140 and 2140

3110   sets variable IX (Independent X) to current value of X variable; redefines X variable as being equal to the negative value of Y; redefines Y variable as being equal to IX (i.e. previous value of X); exits subroutine

3200-10   this subroutine for angles (of a circle) is invoked by 2160

3210   adds 90 to current value of each angle

Error trap

4010   code 52 is the BASIC system code for error caused when a file is not found: in the case of such an error, a message flashes on the screen, the current file is closed, and program resumes at 450. In case of a different error code, program is interrupted, and the error code number is displayed on the screen

Entry from keyboard

5010-5400   this subroutine is invoked by 500

5010-20   displays prompt and expects input for variable KC$ (Keyboard Command)

5030   if command is H (Home) then pen returns to the "home" position, i.e. the lower right corner of the plotter

5040   if command is "end" program exits subroutine and returns to 500

5050-60   if the command entered is not one of the allowed codes, program flashes message and returns to beginning of keyboard subroutine

5100   displays prompt and expects input for X$: this may be an alphanumeric set of characters which may be printed following a P command (given as a value of KC$), or a numeric value which will serve as a the X coordinate

5110   a value "9999" for X$ sends the program back to the prompt

5120   if the numeric value of X$ is greater than 2950 (the maximum width of the plotter), the entry is rejected

5130   if the KC$ (entered earlier) has a value "P" then a command is sent to the plotter, which will print the alphanumeric characters of X$

5140   if KC$ has other values, then the alphanumeric value of X$ is stored as a numeric value

5150   if KC$ has the values B, L, N, Q or S, then the command (KC$) plus the value (X) is sent to the plotter: since no visible action is taken by the plotter at this time, a message flashes on the screen indicating that the entry has taken effect; then the program returns to the beginning of the keyboard subroutine

5210-60   the value Y is treated analogously to X, and the commands I, M and I are executed

5300-20   the value R is treated analogously to X

5330-50   the value S1 is treated analogously to X

5360-80   the value S2 is treated analogously to X

5390   the second part of the circle subroutine is executed (the first part, 2010-2150, is bypassed because the pertinent values of X, Y, R, S1 and S2 have been entered independently of the file pass)

5400   regular end of subroutine

Note. There is no provision in the current version of the program for producing a dotted arc or circle. This can be obtained for now (as in Fig. 2b) by entering in the data file an appropriate sequence of arcs with identical center and radius and progresively higher angles.

8. PROGRAMS

AFP1: Main Program

```
1 REM: AFP1B, Archaeological Floor Plans, Digital Plotting
2 REM: CARNES 1/1, Malibu: Undena Publications, September 1983
20 REM ----------------------------------------------- Fixed definitions - 1
30 DIM N$(20)
40 J=1
50 I=0
60 POKE 150,41
70 LPRINT "F1"
80 ON ERROR GOTO 4000
100 REM ------------------------------------------ Interactive definitions - 2
110 CLS:PRINT "Enter orientation code (v or h)"
120 INPUT OC$
130 IF OC$<>"h" AND OC$<>"v" THEN GOTO 110
140 IF OC$="h" THEN LPRINT "Q0" ELSE LPRINT "Q3"
200 PRINT"Enter coordinates for lower left corner"
210 INPUT "  - X coordinate:";X
220 INPUT "  - Y coordinate:";Y
230 IF OC$="v" THEN GOSUB 3010 ELSE GOTO 240
240 LPRINT "I";X;",";Y
300 CLS:PRINT"Enter scale factor:       "
310 INPUT"  - Operator (/ or *)          ";OP$
320 IF OP$<>"/" AND OP$<>"*" THEN OP$="/":PRINT @70,"/"
330 INPUT"  - Any number 0.1 to 20       ";S
340 IF S >20 OR S<0.1 THEN S=1:PRINT @110,"1"
350 PRINT"Enter step factor for curve"
360 INPUT"  - Any number 0.1 to 5        ";ST
370 IF ST>5 THEN GOTO 360
380 IF ST=0 THEN ST=.5:PRINT @190,".5"
390 PRINT"Enter print size:"
400 INPUT "  - Any number 1 to 25        ";CS
410 IF CS>25 THEN 400
420 IF CS=0 THEN CS=3:PRINT @270,"3"
430 LPRINT "S";CS
440 REM ------------------------------------------------ Main file pass - 3
450 CLS:PRINT"Full files or single entries?"
460 PRINT " - f (full files)"
470 PRINT " - s (single entries)"
480 PRINT " - k (from keyboard)"
485 PRINT " - end (to exit program)"
490 INPUT" ";SE$
500 IF SE$="k" THEN GOSUB 5000
```

```
505 IF SE$="end" THEN END
510 IF SE$<>"f" AND SE$<>"s" AND SE$<>"k" THEN SE$="f":
    PRINT @163,"f"
520 CLS:PRINT "List files to plot, as follows:"
530 PRINT "  filename      - for central memory"
540 PRINT "  CAS:filename - for files on cassette"
550 PRINT "  <CR>          - to exit current pass:"
560 PRINT "If from cassette, check recorder!"
570 I = I+1:IF I>20 THEN I=20:GOTO 600
580 INPUT N$(I):IF N$(I) <> "end" AND N$(I)<>"" THEN GOTO 570
590 I=I-1
600 REM ------------------- Loop (600-840): Data file access - 4
610 IF J>I THEN J=1:I=0:GOTO 450
620 F$ = N$(J)
630 OPEN F$ FOR INPUT AS 1
700 REM ----------Nested loop (700-800): Data file handling - 5
710 LINE INPUT #1, XY$:PR$=LEFT$(XY$,1)
720 KL$="Error in input file! Wait and reenter..."
730 IF PR$<>"*" AND PR$<>"B" AND PR$<>"C" AND PR$<>"D"
    AND PR$<>"H" AND PR$<>"I" AND PR$<>"L" AND PR$<>"M"
    AND PR$<>"N" AND PR$<>"P" AND PR$<>"S" THEN PRINT KL$:
    FOR TL=1 TO 460:NEXT TL:J=J+1:CLOSE 1:GOTO 520
740 IF SE$="s" THEN 750 ELSE 770
750 PRINT "Print "XY$" ?" : INPUT PO$
760 IF PO$="n" THEN 810 ELSE GOTO 770
770 IF PR$="*" THEN GOTO 810
780 GOSUB 1010
790 IF C1$="C" THEN GOTO 810
800 LPRINT XY$
810 IF EOF(1) THEN GOTO 830
820 GOTO 710
830 IF EOF(1) THEN J=J+1:CLOSE 1:GOTO 610
990 END
999 REM ------------------------------- End of main program
1000 REM --------Handling of plotter commands from data file - 6
1010 V=0
1020 C1$=""
1030 V = INSTR(1,XY$,",")
1040 IF V = 0 THEN RETURN
1050 C1$ = MID$(XY$,1,1)
1060 IF C1$="M" THEN GOTO 1100
1070 IF C1$="D" THEN GOTO 1100
1080 IF C1$="I" AND OC$="h" THEN RETURN
1085 IF C1$="I" AND OC$="v" THEN GOSUB 1100:RETURN
1090 IF C1$="C" THEN GOSUB 2010:RETURN ELSE RETURN
1100 C2$=LEFT$(XY$,V-1)
1110 C2$=MID$(C2$,2,LEN(C2$)-1)
1120 C3$=RIGHT$(XY$,LEN(XY$)-V)
1130 X=VAL(C2$): Y=VAL(C3$)
```

```
1140 IF OC$="v" AND C1$<>"I" THEN GOSUB 3100
1145 IF OC$="v" AND C1$="I" THEN GOSUB 3010:GOTO1170
1150 IF OP$="/" THEN X=INT(X/S):Y=INT(Y/S)
1160 IF OP$="*" THEN X=INT(X*S):Y=INT(Y*S)
1170 XY$=C1$+STR$(X)+","+STR$(Y)
1180 RETURN
2000 REM ------------------------------ Circle/Arc subroutine - 7
2010 C2$=LEFT$(XY$,V-1)
2020 C2$=MID$(C2$,2,LEN(C2$)-1)
2030 C3$=MID$(XY$,V+1,LEN(XY$)-V)
2040 V2=INSTR(1,C3$,",")
2050 C4$ =RIGHT$(C3$,LEN(C3$)-V2)
2060 C3$=LEFT$(C3$,V2-1)
2070 V3=INSTR(1,C4$,",")
2080 C5$=RIGHT$(C4$,LEN(C4$)-V3)
2090 C4$=LEFT$(C4$,V3-1)
2100 V4=INSTR(1,C5$,",")
2110 C6$=RIGHT$(C5$,3)
2120 C5$=LEFT$(C5$,3)
2130 X=VAL(C2$):Y=VAL(C3$):R=VAL(C4$):S1=VAL(C5$):S2=VAL(C6$)
2140 IF OC$="v" THEN GOSUB 3100
2150 IF S1=0 AND S2 =360 THEN GOTO 2170 ELSE GOTO 2160
2160 IF OC$="v" THEN GOSUB 3200 ELSE GOTO 2170
2170 IF OP$="/" THEN X=INT(X/S):Y=INT(Y/S):R=INT(R/S)
2180 IF OP$="*" THEN X=INT(X*S):Y=INT(Y*S):R=INT(R*S)
2190 LPRINT "L0"
2500 NR=360/R*2/ST:DR=ATN(1)/45:NN=0
2510 X0=X:Y0=Y:IF S1>S2 THEN NR=-NR
2520 FOR K=S1 TO S2 STEP NR
2530 X=X0+R*COS(K*DR):Y=Y0+R*SIN(K*DR)
2540 IF NN=1 THEN 2560
2550 C$="M":GOSUB 2580
2560 C$="D":GOSUB 2580:NN=1:NEXT
2570 C$="D":X=X0+R*COS(S2*DR):Y=Y0+R*SIN(S2*DR)
2580 LPRINT C$;INT(X);",";INT(Y)
2590 RETURN:RETURN
3000 REM ------------------------------ Orientation subroutines - 8
3010 REM: Origin
3020 XX=2700:IV=X:X=XX-Y:Y=IV:RETURN
3100 REM: Coordinates
3110 IX=X:X=-Y:Y=IX:RETURN
3200 REM: Arc
3210 S1=S1+90:S2=S2+90
3220 RETURN
4000 REM ------------------------------ Error trap - 9
4010 IF ERR=52 THEN PRINT
     "Wrong file name! Wait and reenter ...":
     FOR TL=1 TO 460:NEXT TL:J=J+1:CLOSE 1:RESUME 450
```

CARNES 1,29

```
5000 REM: ------------------------- Entry from keyboard - 10
5010 CLS:PRINT "Parameters for entry from keyboard:"
5020 INPUT " - Command:     ";KC$
5030 IF KC$="H" THEN LPRINT KC$:GOTO 5010
5040 IF KC$="end" THEN RETURN
5050 KL$="Error in input data! Wait and reenter..."
5060 IF KC$<>"B" AND KC$<>"C" AND KC$<>"D" AND KC$<>"I"
     AND KC$<>"L" AND KC$<>"M" AND KC$<>"N" AND KC$<>"P"
     AND KC$<>"Q" AND KC$<>"S" THEN PRINT KL$:
     FOR TL=1 TO 460:NEXT TL:GOTO 5010
5100 INPUT " - Value or X:";X$
5110 IF X$="9999" THEN 5010
5120 IF VAL(X$)>2950 THEN PRINT
     "Value is too high! Reenter...":
     FOR TL=1 TO 230:NEXT TL:GOTO 5100
5130 IF KC$="P" THEN LPRINT KC$;X$:GOTO 5010
5140 IF KC$<>"P" THEN X=VAL(X$)
5150 IF KC$="B" OR KC$="L" OR KC$="N" OR KC$="Q"
     OR KC$="S" THEN LPRINT KC$;X:
     PRINT KC$;X "has been entered":
     FOR TL=1 TO 230:NEXT TL:GOTO 5010
5200 INPUT " -            Y:";Y
5210 IF Y=9999 THEN 5010
5220 IF Y>2950 THEN PRINT
     "Value is too high! Reenter...":
     FOR TL=1 TO 230:NEXT TL:GOTO 5200
5230 X=VAL(X$):IF KC$="I" AND OC$="v" THEN GOSUB 3010 :
     LPRINT "I";X;",";Y:GOTO 5010
5240 IF KC$="I" AND OC$="h" THEN LPRINT "I";X;",";Y:GOTO 5010
5250 IF OC$="v" THEN GOSUB 3100
5260 IF KC$="M" OR KC$="D" THEN LPRINT KC$;X;",";Y:GOTO 5010
5300 INPUT " - radius:      ";R
5310 IF R=9999 THEN 5010
5320 IF R>2000 THEN PRINT
     "Value is too high! Reenter...":
     FOR TL=1 TO 230:NEXT TL:GOTO 5300
5330 INPUT " - arc, start ";S1
5340 IF S1=9999 THEN 5010
5350 IF S1>359 THEN PRINT
     "Value is too high! Reenter...":
     FOR TL=1 TO 230:NEXT TL:GOTO 5330
5360 INPUT " - arc, end    ";S2
5370 IF S2=9999 THEN 5010
5380 IF S2>360 THEN PRINT
     "Value is too high! Reenter...":
     FOR TL=1 TO 230:NEXT TL:GOTO 5360
5390 GOSUB 2160:GOTO 5010
5400 RETURN
```

PL-ED - Plotter Editor (utility program)

The plotter accepts alphanumeric characters only from a BASIC formatted file, a format which is not suitable for entering connected text. The following program allows to do just that: data can be entered as regular text files, and the program PL-ED transforms the text files in BASIC files which can be printed as connected text on the plotter.

```
1 REM: PL-ED: Plotter Editor
5 REM: CARNES 1/1, Malibu: Undena Publications, September 1983
10 LPRINT"F1"
20 LPRINT "S6"
30 X=100
100 PRINT"Name of file to print"
110 INPUT F$
120 PRINT"Lines per page?"
130 INPUT LP
140 OPEN F$ FOR INPUT AS 1
150 FOR I=1 TO LP
160 LINE INPUT #1,L$
170 X=X+100:LPRINT"Q3"
180 LPRINT"M";X;",100"
190 LPRINT"P";L$
200 NEXT I
210 LPRINT"H":X=100
220 PRINT"Paper please! Then, CR"
230 INPUT R1$
240 IF EOF(1) THEN END
250 GOTO 150
260 CLOSE
```

AFP-ED - Archaeological Floor Plans, Editor (utility program)

For a system which does not have a built-in word processor, text files can be created through the editor given here: using BASIC, AFP-ED makes it easy to create text files for later access by the AFP1 program. The version given below is written for a TRS-80 Color Computer.

```
1 REM: AFP-ED - Archaeologgical Floor Plans, Editor
5 REM: CARNES 1/1, Malibu: Undena Publications, September 1983
10 DIM T$(100)
20 PRINT"(E)nter data or (R)ead a file"
30 INPUT R4$
40 IF R4$="E" THEN 100
50 IF R4$="R" THEN PRINT"Name?":INPUT F$:GOTO 330
100 DIM T$(100)
110 I=0
120 I=I+1
130 INPUT T$(I)
140 IF T$(I)<>"END" THEN GOTO 120
150 I=I-1
200 PRINT"Enter name of output file"
210 INPUT F$
220 OPEN "O",#-1,F$
230 FOR J=1 TO I
240 PRINT #-1,T$(J)
250 NEXT J
260 CLOSE
300 PRINT "Read the file?"
310 INPUT R1$
320 IF LEFT$(R1$,1)="N" THEN 300
330 PRINT "Prepare tape then press a key"
340 INPUT R2$
350 K=0
360 OPEN"I",#-1,F$
370 K=K+1
380 INPUT #-1,T$(K)
390 IF EOF(-1) THEN 410
400 GOTO 370
410 CLOSE
420 FOR I=1 TO K
430 PRINT T$(I)
440 NEXT I
450 IF R4$= "R" THEN END
500 PRINT"More?"
510 INPUT R$
520 IF LEFT$(R$,1)="Y" THEN 100 ELSE END
```

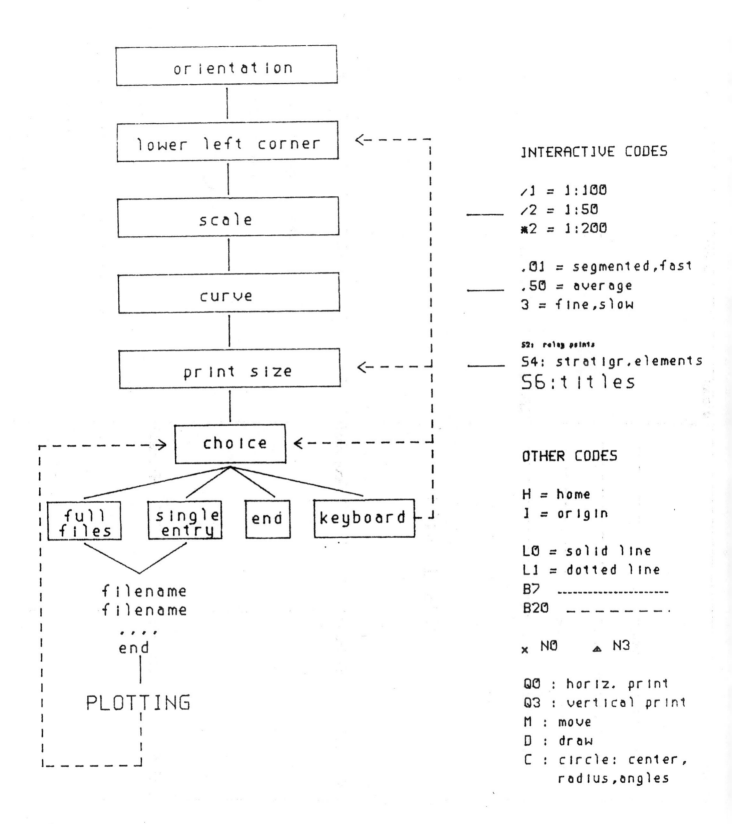

Fig.1. System Flowchart and Summary of Codes

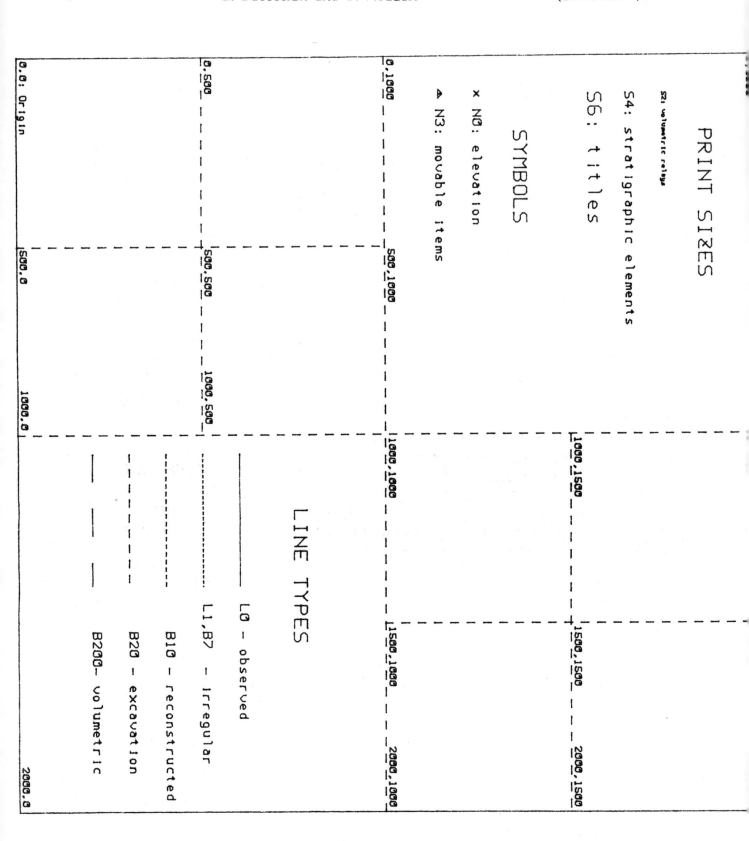

**Fig. 2a. Graphic Symbols on Plotter and
Sample Grid for Horizontal Orientation**

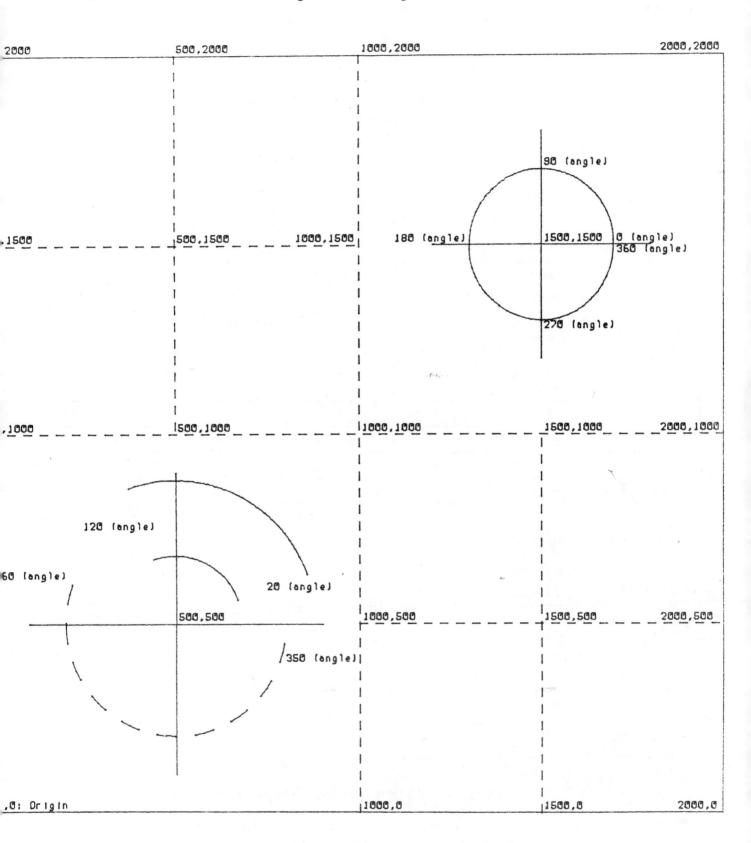

**Fig. 2b. Circles/arcs and
Sample Grid for Vertical Orientation**

IIMAS
1982-FF16

VOLUMETRIC CONTROL INDEX
Excavation Unit F3554

Coordinates for HP used on this sheet

HP	33	N 34999	E 55000		HP	79	N 35759	E 53554
	38	35052	54451			80A	35444	53900

Date Rec. Enc.	Relay No.	Stratigr. Element	Description of Relay	Tie	HP	Tie	HP	Tie	VP	→ N Coordinate	E Coordinate	Elevation	
						Distance				→ N Coordinate	E Coordinate	Elevation	Sfx
12 June 83 DBP	202	T140	Hematite Weight	398	33	374	38	-76	1000	35225	54733	924	
													D
	203	F141	E point at So. Baulk	217	"	364	"	-122	"	35100	54801	878	
													D
	204	"	W point at So. Baulk	135 cms W of R 203						35100	54666	—	D
	205	T141	Cylindrical jar on floor F153	250	80A	623	79	146	"	35512	54145	854	
													D
	206	T142	bifid jar	320	"	607	"	142	"	35640	54163	858	
													D
	207	T143	jar fragment w/ bitumen	233	"	541	"	142	"	35604	54078	858	
													D
13 June 83 DBP	208	T144	bowl	152	"	561	"	143	"	35622	54083	857	
													D
	209	F153, F154	corner	331	"	546	"	—		35820	54031	—	
													D
	210	T145	Islamic strainer	456	H33	799	H34	150	"	35221	54502	850	
													D

Fig. 3a. Volumetric log: Sample entry

Record of ties as measured in the field and derivation of coordinates.
The data for 12 June 83 are shown on the floor plan
in Fig 3b. on the opposite page.

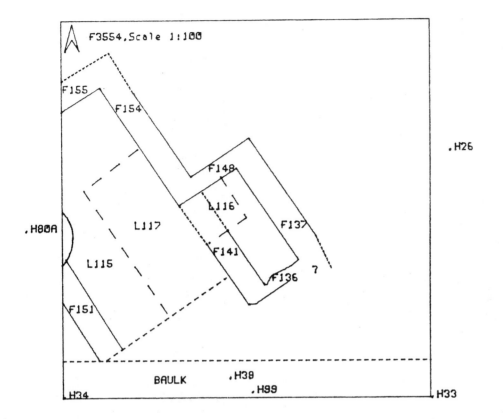

**Current general
floor plan**

This is carried over
from day to day
as a separate file
and is modified
as needed

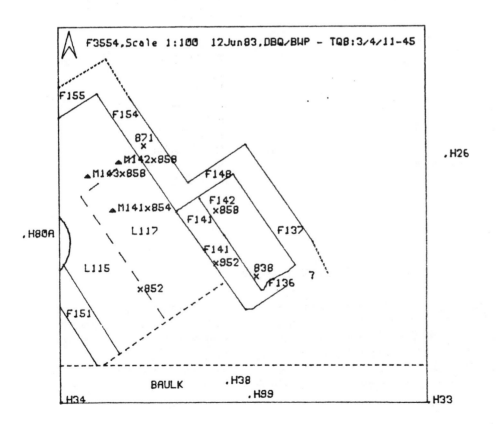

**Entries for
given day**

In this example,
Locus 116 was
excavated
and wall F141
was cleared
completely;
movable items
and elevations
are shown.
On original,
daily entries are
in different color

Fig. 3b. Graphic journal: Sample entry

```
*Excavation Unit Frame          *STCA: Main tablets
L1                              M300,610
B20                             N3
M0,0                            P T55
D1000,0                         M550,370
D1000,1000                      N3
D0,1000                         P T39
D0,0                            M630,600
H                               N3
                                P T165
                                M350,510
*STCA Walls                     N3
L0                              P T1
M80,0                           M280,720
D0,120                          N3
M450,0                          P T23
D400,65                         M310,760
D430,90                         N3
D85,505                         P T63
D100,530                        M490,760
D0,670                          N3
M0,870                          P T60
D70,770                         M490,510
D330,1000                       N3
M780,0                          P T149
D790,10                         M560,560
D660,140                        N3
D620,110                        P T154
D185,650                        M450,410
D560,970                        N3
D970,430                        P T95
D770,240                        M600,380
D890,110                        N3
D1000,210                       P T92
M1000,640                       M750,410
D710,1000                       N3
                                P T94
                                M800,400
*North arrow from 0,0 as origin N3
D50,200                         P T88
D100,0
D50,50
D0,0
```

Fig. 4. Data file input

The floor plan on Fig. 5 (opposite page) was plotted from the files listed above. (The listing was produced on the plotter by means of the utility program PL-ED given above in Section 8.) The filenames were entered all at once, and the plotter executed the commands in the propr sequence.

Note that the file "STCA Walls" is exactly the same that was used to produce the small upper right square of the floor plan on Fig.6: only the scale factor before execution of the program was different ("*2" for Fig. 5 and "/2" for Fig. 6).

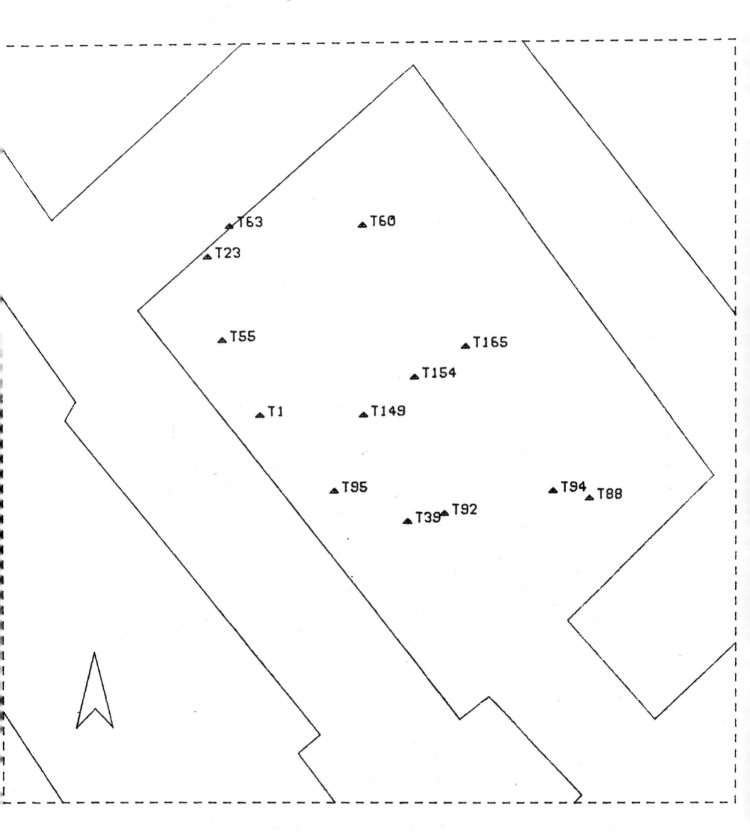

Fig. 5. Sample Floor Plan, Scale 1:50
(Archive Room of Puzurum, with location of main tablets)

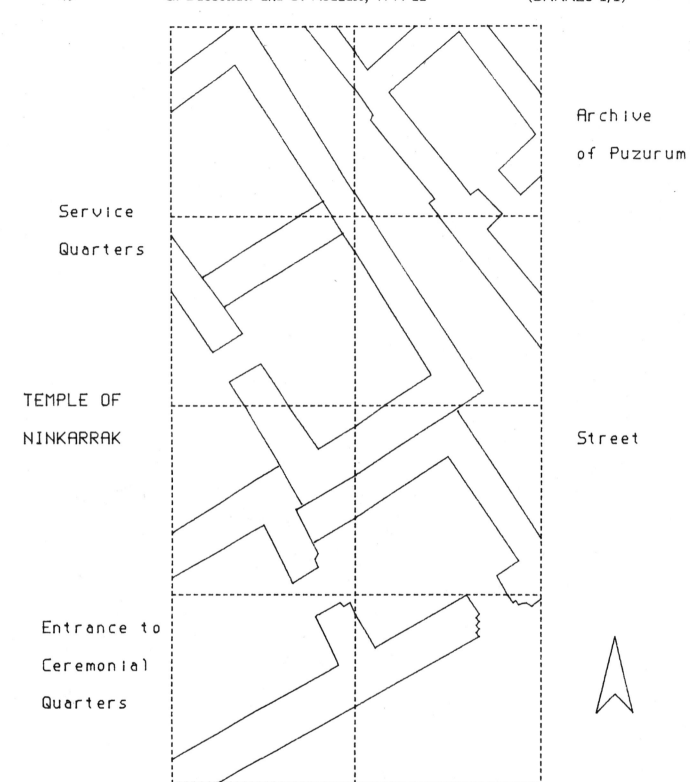

Archive

of Puzurum

Service

Quarters

TEMPLE OF

NINKARRAK

Street

Entrance to

Ceremonial

Quarters

Fig. 6. Sample Floor Plan, Scale 1:200
(House of Puzurum and temple of Ninkarrak, early phase)